CYCLE A GOSPEL TEXTS

LIFE IN HEAVEN'S KINGDOM

SERMONS FOR
SUNDAYS AFTER
PENTECOST
(LAST THIRD)

D. WAYNE
BURKETTE

C.S.S. Publishing Co., Inc.
Lima, Ohio

LIFE IN HEAVEN'S KINGDOM

Copyright © 1989 by
The C.S.S. Publishing Company, Inc.
Lima, Ohio

All rights reserved. No part of this publication may be reproduced, stored in a retrieval system, or transmitted in any form or by any means, electronic, mechanical, photocopying, recording, or otherwise, without the prior permission of the publisher. Inquiries should be addressed to: The C.S.S. Publishing Company, Inc., 628 South Main Street, Lima, Ohio 45804.

9855 / ISBN 1-55673-130-2 PRINTED IN U.S.A.

Table of Contents

Preface			5
Lectionary Preaching After Pentecost			6
Proper 22[1] Pentecost 20[2] Ordinary Time 27[3]	Matthew 21:33-43	Possession is Nine Tenths of the Fall	9
Proper 23 Pentecost 21 Ordinary Time 28	Matthew 22:1-14[1,3] Matthew 22:1-10 (11-14)[2]	The Gift That Claims Our Response	15
Proper 24 Pentecost 22 Ordinary Time 29	Matthew 22:15-22[1] Matthew 22:15-21[2,3]	The Things That Are God's	21
Proper 25 Pentecost 23 Ordinary Time 30	Matthew 22:34-46[1] Matthew 22:34-40 (41-46)[2] Matthew 22:34-40[3]	The Love God Wants	27
Proper 26 Pentecost 24[a],26[b] Ordinary Time 31	Matthew 23:1-12[1,2b,3] Matthew 23:1-13[2a]	Who Is Greatest Among You . . .	33
Proper 27 Ordinary Time 32	Matthew 25:1-13	Life in the Meantime	39
Proper 28 Pentecost 25 Ordinary Time 33	Matthew 25:14-30	In Defense of the One-Talent Servant	45
Pentecost 27	Matthew 24:1-14	Promise or Threat?	51
Proper 29 Christ the King Ordinary Time 34	Matthew 25:31-46 (Ezekiel 34:11-16, 23-24)	God's Safety Net	57
Reformation Day/ Reformation Sunday[2]	John 8:31-36	The Freedom of Necessity	65
All Saints' Day All Saints' Sunday[1,2]	Matthew 5:1-12	When the Poor Become Rich	69

[1]Common Lectionary
[2]Lutheran Lectionary
[3]Roman Catholic Lectionary

For
Nancy,
Allison, and Amanda

Preface

The Gospel texts of the Common Lectionary for the last third of the Pentecost season (Cycle A) are not unified by a single theme. They are, however, alike in that each in its own way points to the character of a life lived under God's rule of grace and justice.

Five of the texts are parables about the Kingdom of God, and all of the others give direction and correction to persons who would be its participants. Perhaps out of respect for the ancient Hebrew prohibition against speaking the name of God, Matthew's Gospel frequently refers to God's Kingdom as the "kingdom of heaven." But Matthew's reference need not be understood as entirely eschatological.

The sermons in this volume grow out of a conviction that whatever else the Kingdom of Heaven may be, it is also a condition of life which can be experienced here and now in part, and in its fullness in the life to come. Thus, the life we live now and the life which yet shall be are truly one life — the life of Heaven's Kingdom.

Lectionary Preaching After Pentecost

Virtually all pastors who make use of the sermons in this book will find their worship life and planning shaped by one of two lectionary series. Most mainline Protestant denominations, along with clergy of the Roman Catholic Church, have now approved — either for provisional or official use — the three-year Common (Consensus) Lectionary. This family of denominations include United Methodist, Presbyterian, United Church of Christ, and Disciples of Christ.

Lutherans and Roman Catholics, while testing the Common Lectionary on a limited basis at present, follow their own three-year cycle of texts. While there are divergences between the Common and Lutheran/Roman Catholic systems, the gospel texts show striking parallels, with few text selections evidencing significant differences. Virtually all the gospel texts included in this book will, therefore, be applicable to worship and preaching planning for clergy following either lectionary.

A significant divergence does occur, however, in the method by which specific gospel texts are assigned to specific calendar days. The Common and Roman Catholic lectionaries accomplish this by counting backwards from Christ the King (Last Sunday after Pentecost), discarding "extra" texts from the front of the list; Lutherans follow the opposite pattern, counting forward from The Holy Trinity, discarding "extra" texts at the end of the list.

The following index will aid the user of this book in matching the right text to the right Sunday during the "Pentecost Half" of the church year (days listed here include only those appropriate to this book's contents):

Common (Consensus) Lectionary   **Lutheran/ Roman Catholic Lectionary**

Text Designation	Calendar	
Proper 22	October 2-8	Pentecost 20/ Ordinary Time 27
Proper 23	October 9-15	Pentecost 21/ Ordinary Time 28
Proper 24	October 16-22	Pentecost 22/ Ordinary Time 29

Common (Consensus) Lectionary		**Lutheran/Roman Catholic Lectionary**
Text Designation	*Calendar*	
Proper 25	October 23-29	Pentecost 23/ Ordinary Time 30
Proper 26	October 30 — November 5	Pentecost 24/ Ordinary Time 31
Proper 27	November 6-12	Pentecost 25/ Ordinary Time 32 Pentecost 26/ Ordinary Time 33
Proper 28	November 13-19	Pentecost 27
Christ the King	November 20-26	Christ the King
Reformation Sunday	Last Sunday in October	Reformation Sunday
All Saints' Sunday	First Sunday in November	All Saints' Sunday

Matthew 21:33-43   **Proper 22 (C)**
Pentecost 20 (L)
Ordinary Time 27 (RC)

Possession is Nine Tenths of the Fall

Graham Greene writes in one of his novels, "If a man loves a place enough he doesn't need to possess it; it's enough for him to know that it is safe and unaltered . . . ." (*The Tenth Man,* New York, Pocket Books, 1986, p. 89.)

The trouble is that we never seem to be able to love quite enough, at least not enough to be delivered from the unhappy desire to own our lives and almost everything that touches them. It seems so often that nothing pleases some people more than the feeling that life is like putty in their hands, ready for whatever molding and shaping they desire at the moment. Unfortunately, as the Parable of the Wicked Tenants illustrates, the inevitable end to this deadly desire is some kind of self-destruction.

Imagine it in the way Jesus told it in his parable. The tenants of the vineyard have it all. Everything they need is provided — hedge, wine press, watch tower. It's all there for them to tend and use, and it's fair to say, to enjoy. There is not even the pressure of a supervisor looking over their shoulders, since the householder has left the country. They are on their own. It's all theirs to care for, to keep safe and productive.

But, so the story goes, they blow it! Enjoying, taking care of, and working in the vineyard are not enough. The tenants want more. They want to *own* it. Their desire runs through stages of increasing greed. They kill the servants whom the householder sends to collect the rent. They defy the householder at every turn, until finally, no alternative is left to the householder except to send the son. "My son," thinks the householder, "will command their respect; they will listen to him."

But they don't. Instead, they kill the son as they murdered the servants, and all for the same reason: that they might have his inheritance. With the son out of the way, and the householder away from the country for such a long time as to lose rights to the property, the whole vineyard will be theirs. Hedge, wine press, tower — all will be theirs, to do with as *they* please. No more orders from some absentee landlord. They themselves will be householders and have complete control. The future will belong to them.

And that's the way so much of our trouble, humanly speaking, begins. Ever since Adam and Eve set out to possess the fruit of the forbidden tree, at the heart of much of the unhappiness and sorrow in life is an all-consuming need to be in control, to be our own gods.

Mind you, the need to possess things is not intrinsically evil. Specialists in child development tell us that one of the essential steps in personality growth is a child's ability to distinguish what belongs to him or her from the surrounding environment. Infants learn very early that the hand or foot they glimpse occasionally is theirs and not part of the crib. Later on, children learn, or should, that property which belongs to another person is not theirs for the taking. The Old Testament commandment against stealing recognizes that ownership is a right meant to be respected.

But like so many other human rights and desires which are not in and of themselves evil, the need to possess frequently exceeds its limits. The necessity to own some things can become the compulsion to own legions of things far beyond what may be useable or helpful. The result? Relationships suffer. Intended to rest on foundations of love and mutual respect, relationships can become terribly possessive as they also become extensions of the desire to control — parents who keep trying to own their children; husbands or wives who seek to possess their spouses; powerful nations which repeatedly impose their visions of the world and its resources upon poorer and less powerful peoples. Unrestrained desire is at the heart of more problems than most of us want to admit.

In Joseph Conrad's classic story *Heart of Darkness,* the character of Mr. Kurtz stands out as the epitome of unbridled desire to possess life. Kurtz is the manager of a jungle trading post, in the employ of a late nineteenth-century English company. He ships more ivory to the Company than do all the other managers put together. Everything around him — people, land, and especially ivory — is his for the taking. He is rising to the top of the corporate ladder fast when suddenly illness overtakes him, and even the seemingly omnipotent Kurtz is unable to thwart the disease's devastation. Marlowe, who has been sent by the Company to replace the dying despot, watches as a steamboat is loaded with Kurtz's last shipment of ivory, and reflects upon the dying despot's legacy.

> *You should have heard him say, 'My ivory.' Oh yes, I heard him. 'My Intended, my ivory, my station, my river, my _____.' Everything belonged to him — but that was a trifle. The thing was to know what he belonged to, how many powers of darkness claimed him for their own.*
> (Joseph Conrad, *Heart of Darkness*, New York, W. W. Norton and Company, Inc., 1971, 1963, p. 49.)

Conrad's story illustrates dramatically how the possessor can become the possessed, destroyed by the very desire that motivated his achievement.

Even religion, meant to be a means of acknowledging God's ownership and dominion over all life, can be perverted into a subtle human effort to bend the divine will to fit our own purposes, and thus a way of possessing God and God's favor. Perhaps it was such perversion of religion which was uppermost in Jesus' mind as he told the Parable of the Wicked Tenants. Many biblical scholars believe that this was the last parable Jesus told. And, although it has been regarded generally as a reference to Judaism's rejection of Jesus as Messiah and his eventual death, surely it is more than that. Could it be that in what was probably his final parable concerning the Kingdom which he had come to proclaim, Jesus was cautioning all who would follow him not to misunderstand their roles in that Kingdom? The Spirit and the gifts are surely ours, but ours to use, not to own. Christian faith and its expressions are not human instruments for compelling God, but divine gifts for use in glorifying God and loving people.

It's easy, though, for the practice of religion to become proud and arrogant, possessive of its status. We have experienced over the last decade the emergence of a variety of highly possessive and arrogant religious movements and people, both in Christianity and in other traditions. Even as the so-called religious right gained voice and political clout in the United States, so did right wing Islam in Iran and in other parts of the Islamic world. Such religious dogmatism is by definition highly possessive. It reaches to own and articulate *the* truth, *the* way a person (or nation) should live, *the* principles by which even God lives, moves, and has his being. One can almost hear in the rhetoric of dogmatic religion, be it Christian or Islamic, the voices of the vineyard tenants saying, "The inheritance of the faith belongs to us alone. We know and claim what is rightly ours." Such an attitude is to be regarded more with pity than with judgment, for it always seems to self-destruct when finally it runs its course.

There is a legend about a simple man who was lifted from the gutter and magically granted three wishes. First he wished for material goods and forthwith became very rich. Then he wished for understanding and soon became very wise. At last he used his third wish to express his desire to become as God, and immediately he found himself back in the gutter.

So it was with the wicked tenants. Dissatisfied with their role as stewards and not owners, they eventually lost the very vineyard which supported them. The tenants of the vineyard are most to be pitied. We can only hope and pray for the innocents who always suffer in their self-destruction.

Over against and pleading with the character of a possessive, dogmatic attitude stands the teaching and example of Jesus. It is no coincidence that most of the conflict Jesus experienced was with persons and institutions who were certain that they were right, that they knew exactly what God willed and what God did not, that the spiritual vineyard of their day belonged exclusively to them. It is no surprise that when a gospel of grace meets head-on with dogmatic religion, the inevitable result is conflict. God's grace is always a lurking threat to the conviction that people must earn salvation through ownership of the truth and control of the one and only way. God's grace opens the gates of the Kingdom to those who, from the possessors' point of view, do not deserve it. The gospel of grace denies our ownership of anything and boldly proclaims that even faith itself is a gift.

So what makes God's claim upon life the good news that it is? Nothing less than the mystery that the God who owns all is also the God who loves all. In that mystery we experience the joy and freedom which come with the assurance that our lives belong totally to God, God who loves us completely. We discover that joy and wholeness of life consist not in control but in commitment to the always larger and greater cause of the Kingdom. We sense the beauty of life lived by grace rather than grasp. Having abandoned the deadly desire to possess life and be our own gods, we are greeted by a remarkable serendipity — the abundant life that we could never seize by our own strength is given to us free and clear. The tenants of God's vineyard are revealed to be also God's children, "heirs of God and fellow heirs with Christ." (Romans 8:17) That's news so good as to be hard for some to believe.

If only the tenants of the vineyard had heard it. They were already children of the householder. The vineyard was their inheritance all the time.

Matthew 22:1-14 (C, RC)
Matthew 22:1-10 (11-14) (L)

Proper 23 (C)
Pentecost 21 (L)
Ordinary Time 28 (RC)

The Gift That Claims Our Response

Some of the gifts we receive have a way of dramatically altering our lifestyles. Remember the day a well-meaning friend gave your children that cute little puppy? No household can just accept a new puppy and go on with life as usual. Certain changes are inevitable.

Or to consider even more profound lifestyle changes, think of what happens when a baby is born into a family. Long gone are the nights of eight hours of uninterrupted sleep; soon the refrigerator is filled with jars of strained beets; and you hardly finish congratulating yourself for seeing light at the end of the tunnel of childhood years, when you read a front page article on the astronomical costs of four years of college.

Don't misunderstand. The gift is precious beyond all measure, but there's no denying that it's a gift which calls forth some serious, well-considered responses from the recipients.

Jesus' parables of the wedding feast and the guest without a wedding garment call us to consider a similar kind of gift — one that claims our response, one that necessitates adjustment in our styles of life. The gift is the invitation of Christ to participate in the Kingdom of God; it's the gracious offer of Jesus to seek and enjoy that condition of life wherein faith and hope and love are celebrated and practiced.

Jesus said that the offer to participate in this Kingdom is like being invited to a marriage feast. Some people make all kinds of excuses for not accepting the invitation, but the truth is they aren't interested. They don't want to be bothered. Perhaps they know that if they accept the invitation they will be obligated to respond appropriately, and they have other priorities.

So the king who's giving the marriage feast, not wanting to see the food wasted, invites anybody and everybody. He decides that if his so-called "friends" will not come, then he will open up the guest list to anyone willing to show up.

As people often do when there's a free meal, they arrive in large numbers. And what a feast it is! No Big Macs and fries, but ox tail soup and prime rib.

Shortly after the guests arrive the king makes his appearance, thinking to himself, "These may not be the people I thought would be here, but at least these *did* come. They have saved me from the disappointment of a full table and nobody with whom to enjoy it." So the king begins to mingle among the guests and extend his greetings as any good host should do.

As he shakes first this hand and that one, he comes upon a fellow who hasn't bothered to put on clean clothes and dress appropriately for the occasion. The king stops in front of this fellow and demands, "Friend, how did you get in here without the proper attire?" A hush hurries through the hall as though E. F. Hutton had spoken. But the poor fellow has no answer, so without hesitation the king has the man tossed out on his ear. Jesus concludes the story with a comment about many being called but few being chosen. It is a hard saying.

For years this parable troubled me, because I didn't understand it. It seemed to be a puzzling story of ruthless judgment, where a poor soul was chastized unmercifully for a relatively minor breach of etiquette. Surely the king overreacted. After all, we have all found ourselves inappropriately dressed on at least one or two occasions. Besides, the Gospel says that we shouldn't be making judgments about others on the basis of appearances.

But some time ago, further research into the social customs of Jesus' day brought to light a fact that has altered my understanding of the parable. I still find it bothersome, but now it troubles me because I think I *do* understand it!

In Jesus' day, when a king or any influential person gave a marriage feast, the host also provided wedding garments for all who attended. These garments, probably loose-fitting tunics worn over regular clothing, were distributed to the dinner guests as they arrived. The host's only expectation was that the invited guests would slip the garments on before entering the banquet hall. This bit of social protocol, fully understood and appreciated by the people who first heard Jesus tell the story, puts the whole parable in a different light. (Richard Carl Hoefler, *The Divine Trap*, Lima, Ohio, C.S.S. Publishing Co., 1980, p. 119).

The ill-clad guest who was brusquely ushered out of the hall was not a victim after all. He was, to put it bluntly, an ingrate who took what he could get but refused to express any gratitude or respect for what he had received. He had been honored with a rare and precious gift — the opportunity to be part of a royal fest — but he refused to change clothes and put on the appropriate dress provided by the host. Instead of a person victimized by a meager wardrobe, we find a person who was callously indifferent to the need to respond with respect and gratitude for what he had been given so graciously.

The point is one of both good news and bad news. The good news is that we are all invited into the Kingdom of God to join the party. The bad news is that some of us will be ashamed of the way we look when we get there. We will be ashamed, not because our appearance is unacceptable, but because we took the grace and generosity of God for granted. Instead of responding with appropriate changes in our lifestyles and actions, we will have tried to enjoy the feast of God's grace on our own terms, without the bother of putting on a wedding garment.

The invitation into that condition of life called the Kingdom of Heaven always claims our response. God's grace is free, but it is not cheap. We have a need to respond to what we have been given and to do so in ways that show our thanksgiving for the Giver of all good gifts.

The connection between this parable and the nature of the church is inescapable. In my study is a nineteenth-century print entitled "Saving the Lost." It is an artist's representation of the mission of the church to rescue those who are perishing in a sea of sin. A poor soul, awash in an ocean and clinging for life to a floating timber, is being tossed a lifeline by those on board the ship of the church. The implicit message is that if only the poor soul can be brought on board in time, salvation will have been gained.

Our Lord's tragic story of a guest without a wedding garment raises some disturbing questions about that understanding of the church's calling. Being on the ship, being a member, being inside the banquet hall is not sufficient. In fact, it's only the first step, an important step, but only the first of many yet to come. The real issue for us has to do with remaining open to the continuing change and growth which God expects in return for the gift of salvation.

Richard Carl Hoefler has put it succinctly this way, "Salvation is not a product we possess but a process in which we participate." (*Ibid.*, p. 120) It's a process of receiving daily of the abundance of God's forgiveness and all God's good gifts, and responding daily to what we have received. We respond with the giving of ourselves and all we have in service and openness to God and our neighbor.

The wonder of the process is deepened by the realization that God never expects us to respond with what we don't have. God doesn't expect me to sing solos in church (and for that we can all be eternally grateful). God doesn't expect you or me to add a twenty-fifth hour to every day or an eighth day to every week in order to have the time to do God's work and serve our neighbor. God doesn't expect you or me to borrow money in order to give it away.

It is of God's nature however to expect of us a proportionate share of what each of us has been given. That means we respond not as an afterthought with leftover time, leftover energy, leftover money, but we respond with what the Bible calls our firstfruits — a response off the top of our lives, not from leftovers. In other words, God asks only for the wedding garment of faith and love to be put on by all who come to the party. And the garment itself is God's own gift.

I would like to think that all of us are eager to put on those garments of grateful response, and that most of us have so clothed ourselves. But if we have put them on, we still must be attentive to the garment's condition. It's easy to become so involved with enjoyment of the feast through the years of our lives that we forget to check the garment of our response every now and then to see whether it's wearing a little thin here or there, or whether some repair or mending is needed. It's comfortable to lean back and think, "I've done my part; I've given my fair share; I've used my talents," assuming that we can live off the interest of faith deposits made years ago.

The Gospel never speaks of any such sense of completion, not in this life. Our response is never finished; it only changes character from time to time as our circumstances change. The need to respond is equally strong in every stage of life. The feast of the kingdom has commenced, and invitations are extended every day. And along with the invitation, God provides the garment of response. God even gives the Spirit who urges us continually, "Put it on!"

Matthew 22:15-22 (C) *Proper 24 (C)*
Matthew 22:15-21 (L, RC) *Pentecost 22 (L)*
Ordinary Time 29 (RC)

The Things That Are God's

Truth is where you find it, and not always where you expect.

Remember the old story about a chicken and a pig who wanted to show their gratitude for all the farmer's care and protection? The chicken decided that, given the limitations placed upon them, the best they could do was to provide the farmer with a delicious ham and eggs breakfast. So the chicken told the pig what she had decided. The pig responded, "For you, a ham and eggs breakfast is a gesture of great generosity, but for me, it is an act of total commitment!"

The truth is that commitment in the religious sense is nothing less than the complete giving of oneself to God. Generosity follows commitment, but commitment comes first. And commitment is the subject of the Gospel for today.

Matthew says that an uncommon coalition of Pharisees and Herodians approached Jesus to ask him a loaded question, one designed to have no answer except a wrong one. So, like reporters encircling a presidential candidate, they pressed him, "Is it lawful to pay taxes to Caesar or not?" Of course it was lawful in Roman jurisprudence, but religious law was uppermost in their minds. Judaism was divided on the question, thus the aim of the inquiry was to force Jesus to take sides in a no-win argument. Jesus had spoken harsh words against the Pharisees.

They were threatened and had appeared vulnerable in the public eye. So, they figured that if they could entangle Jesus in a controversy over Roman taxes, the heat would be off them. Somewhere they learned that the best defense is a good offense.

But Jesus' answer did what was characteristic of his responses to loaded questions. He carefully avoided being victimized by their malice and, at once, challenged them to a new faith-understanding.

"Show me the money for the tax," he said. And they brought him the coin of the realm. "Whose image and inscription do you see on the coin?" Well, of course everybody knew it was Caesar's image. It was as obvious as the picture of the President hanging in the Post Office. "Then render to Caesar the things that are Caesar's," Jesus commanded, "and to God the things that are God's."

When the Pharisees and Herodians heard Jesus' answer they marveled, and walked away in astonishment. And well they should have been amazed. For Pharisees, above most other Jews, knew the Scriptures. And the Scriptures made it clear, in the very first book, that God's image was upon only one thing in all the universe. God's image was impressed, not on the coins of the empire, but upon human life itself. "Then God said, 'Let us make man in our image, after our likeness' .... So God created man in his image . . . male and female he created them." (Genesis 1:26, 27)

The implication of Jesus' command to render to God what rightfully belonged to God was obvious to all who heard it. Give your coins to Caesar when you must, but give *yourselves* to God. Caesar may compel you to be generous with your tax money, whether cheerfully or begrudgingly, but God's claim calls for complete commitment. Caesar's image may be on your coins, but God's image is on you.

The wonder in Jesus' answer is that it calls forth an examination of all our commitments and loyalties. It suggests that all our earthly loyalties are penultimate and must be reevaluated continually in light of an ultimate commitment to God.

No one seriously denies that we all have legions of loyalties. Sometimes there are too many for our own good. I remember watching a film a few years ago in which a scene opened to show two puppeteers arguing over who would control the strings tied to a marionette on the stage below them. As they argued, one tried to wrest the strings from the other. The result was predictable. The puppet was pulled and thrown this way and that across the stage, as first one puppeteer and then the other pulled the string to an arm or leg, hand or foot.

Our many loyalties and commitments can do the same to us. We may feel that the strings of power and persuasion tied to us need only be tugged a bit, and then we have to move as they direct. The company we work for, the government we live under, the family we belong to, the possessions we own (moreso, the one's we're still paying for) — all these things exercise varying degrees of control over our lives. To a large extent they determine how we spend our time, our money, our energy, our being. It isn't rare at all these days for people to be pulled in so many different directions that they jump and jerk across the stage of life, often feeling helplessly out of control.

Our problem is that there are too many Caesars before which we stand accountable. It's impossible to please them all. Rendering to Caesar what is Caesar's is more than some folk feel they can handle.

Now Jesus complicates the picture further by commanding that even what we render to Caesar must be offered in the larger context of an ultimate, all-inclusive commitment to God.

Consider it this way. Our lives are not like rows of compartments, work here, family there, God here, money there, each neatly separated from the other. Tremendous energy can be expended keeping all the compartments properly partitioned so that one doesn't impinge on another. Instead, our lives are like one huge circus tent filled with all kinds of activities, some enjoyable, some not so pleasant, some happy, some sad. But the tent within which all this activity takes place is none other than our devotion and allegiance to God. That means that over and surrounding our every decision, every choice, every loyalty, every responsibility, is a complete commitment of ourselves to the way and will of God.

"Render to God the things that are God's" — the only conclusion to draw from this commandment is to give ourselves to God first, before anything else. Then all other loyalties must be given or withheld subject to the direction and correction of that first loyalty. Only then can commitment to God become a kind of gravitational force which gives us some stability and balance when all the strings on our lives are being pulled this way and that.

Mind you, commitment to God is no guarantee of comfort — material or emotional. It produces its own tension, because it demands that we constantly re-examine all our other loyalties to be certain that they are in their proper places. And, if any be discovered which demand of us what rightly belongs to God, or which require of us a betrayal of our first loyalty, then we must obey God first. Whether to country, employer, or even family, all our commitments are subject to the divine claim upon our lives.

H. Richard Niebhur once wrote that "faith in God involves us in a permanent revolution of the mind and heart." (*Radical Monotheism and Western Culture,* New York, Harper and Row, 1960, p. 126) That's what total commitment to God requires and produces. Exciting and challenging? Yes. Comfortable? Never.

Matthew concludes this little slice from the life of Jesus by noting that when the Pharisees and Herodians had heard Jesus' astonishing comeback, they left him and went away. Foiled in their attempt to embroil him in a controversy, they left, I suspect, having entangled themselves in an inner controversy. If they took Jesus' words to heart and found in them the truth that was surely there, they had to ask of themselves some troubling questions. "Have I rendered to God my life, which life bears His image and likekess?" "Have I surrendered to Caesar what rightfully belongs to God?" Have I lost, God forbid, the ability to feel the tension between my fidelity to

God and all my other obligations?" I suspect that those concerns were on at least a few minds.

Tennyson has a relevant verse concerning the knights of Arthur's Round Table:

> *For good ye are and bad, and like to coins,*
> *Some true, some light, but everyone of you*
> *Stamped with the image of the King.*
> (*Interpreter's Bible*, Vol. 7, Abingdon Press, 1951, p. 520).

So we are. Stamped with the image of God. The Pharisees and Herodians may have left Jesus, but I doubt that his words ever left them. And neither will they leave us.

"Render to God the things that are God's."

Matthew 22:34-46 (C)
Matthew 22:34-40 (41-46) (L)
Matthew 22:34-40 (RC)

Proper 25 (C)
Pentecost 23 (L)
Ordinary Time 30 (RC)

The Love God Wants

Judging from current fads in vocabulary, it seems that most of us think that life is too complicated, or at least, more complicated than it needs to be. One clue is the frequency of the words, "basic" and "basically" in our speech.

"The basic idea of the proposal is . . . ."

"Basically, how do you see the situation?"

And most all of us have given in to the fashion of creating nouns out of adjectives as we express the need to "get back to the basics" in everything from education to economics.

We long for clarity and understanding of the fundamental matters of living. As our lives become more and more complex, we yearn for simple, easy-to-cope with issues and ideas. But life seldom cooperates in our search for simplicity. To some extent the growth of religious fundamentalism in our society reflects that search for simple answers to complex questions, for a way of understanding God and the religious life which does not have to grapple with the challenges of science and philosophy.

Matthew's Gospel says that the Pharisees, having heard that Jesus had dumbfounded the Sadducees, seized the opportunity to hand Jesus their own test of orthodoxy. One of them questioned Jesus as to what was the most important Commandment in the law. Jesus' answer cut through layers of religious laws and ordinances and went straight to the heart of Judaism.

He recited Israel's ancient creed, the "shema," and coupled it with a succinct summary of the Levitical code. And, lest that sound complicated, his answer was "basically" this: "Love God completely, with all your being. That's the first Commandment. And just as important, there is a second Commandment — love your neighbor as much as you love yourself."

With those two teachings, Jesus crystallized centuries of theology and articulated the essence of what life in covenant with God is all about. Some would even say that these Commandments are the very hinges on which the door to heaven swings, and that the matter of whether or not that door opens to any person is somehow related to these twin commands. In other words, Christian faith and practice doesn't get any more basic than this, "Love God completely, and love your neighbor as yourself."

The willingness of Jesus to give the Pharisees an answer is a reminder that some aspects of faith and practice are indeed more important than others. And the profound brevity of his answer seems to say that the list of those criteria fundamental to a Christian's lifestyle is short, certainly shorter than many who call themselves "fundamentalists" would have us believe.

One of the prayers in our Litany petitions God to "deliver us from fanaticism." It would be interesting, and perhaps amusing, to know what images race through our minds when we make that prayer. For some it would be gloom and doom prophets walking through the city streets calling for repentance. Others might envision door to door callers handing out tracts and pamphlets. Or maybe we think of the "Moonies" selling roses down at the corner.

Put simply, a fanatic is a person who forgets what is truly important and thus beings to major in something minor. Fanaticism results when something of small importance becomes for a person the whole of life. Though sports fans are not necessarily fanatics, the word "fan" is short for the same. And "fanatical" does seem to be an apt description of at least some sports fans. We can agree on that because all of us know that basketball, football, golf, or any other sport is not the most important thing in life, much less the whole of life. But when we act as though our team's winning *is* the most important thing in life, then we have stepped across some invisible line between being a "fan" and being a "fanatic."

The fact that Jesus was willing to identify love for God and neighbor as weightier than any other biblical teaching or precept serves to remind us all of what is truly important in living. Finer points of doctrine are important sometimes, but they are not *the main thing*. The main thing in living a life after the way of Jesus is to embody the love which God wants of us, for God and for neighbor.

These twin towers of religious law as Jesus summarized them suggest also that the religious life has both inward and outward dimensions. Almost twenty-five years ago, Elizabeth O'Conner wrote a book about the life and ministry of The Church of the Savior in Washington, D.C. She documented how the people of that church had tried to achieve a balance between the contemplative life of spiritual growth and nurture and the practical life of social action. She entitled her book, *Journey Inward, Journey Outward* (New York, Harper and Row Publishers, 1968). That is also an appropriate title for the implied conclusion in the great Commandments. It suggests the balance called for by the Letter of James, the balance between faith and works. Love for God, which is the first command from our Lord, is but spiritual smugness unless it issues forth in a lifestyle which seeks love, justice, and peace for our neighbors, whether neighbors next door or in another hemisphere. No one can take the two great commandments seriously and be content with *just* a life of worship, prayer, and study, or *just* a life of social action and humanistic thought. The love God wants includes both.

Finally, the two great Commandments as Jesus identifies them present us with an impossible possibility. That is, the kind of love they command is at once our practical duty and responsibility and an ideal beyond our reach. To love God *completely* and to love one's neighbor as *oneself* is a mission impossible.

The moment we become self-conscious of our love, either for God or neighbor, we lose that essential sponteneity and selflessness required of pure love. The very moment I think to myself, "I have demonstrated my love for God in worship today," the emphasis begins to move from "worship" and "God" to "I" and "my." The second I begin to feel that twinge of pride in having assisted my neighbor, love is diminished. Love for God or for neighbor is never immune to the fatal disease of self-righteousness; to the contrary, it is as susceptible to it as is obedience to any of the other Commandments, maybe more so.

The impossible possibility of the dual love for God and neighbor thus serves to cast us anew upon God's grace and mercy. As our love, feeble as it is, continually falls short of the complete and selfless love Jesus commanded, we experience that essential inability and ineptness which is basic to our nature, and which makes us dependent upon a merciful and gracious God to do for us what we cannot do for ourselves.

There is only one act of perfect obedience to the two great commandments, and that is the life and death of Jesus. On him all the law and the prophets truly depend, for in him they all come together and realize their fulfillment in both purpose and obedience. Only Christ loved God with all heart, soul, and mind; only Christ loved his neighbor as himself.

Sinclair Lewis' character, Elmer Gantry, comes to mind by way of contrast. Elmer Gantry's revivalistic sermons on love were silky smooth, oozing with sentiment and emotion, and they moved people to tears and generosity. But, Gantry was a charletan, a manipulator of people and their commitment. His words were hollow, self-serving, and deceitful. He captivated people by eloquently parading before them the beauty and sentimentality of love, and exhorting them to be more loving; but there was little love in Gantry himself, only an all-consuming desire to build a religious empire and garner its fame and fortune. In the end, Gantry perished, and with him the hopes of those whom he manipulated.

In dramatic contrast, Jesus was the personification of the very thing he commanded. Thus, persons who are in Christ, those in whom Christ's Spirit dwells, are delivered from their own inability to love completely by the One who was Perfect Love.

Life is complicated, and following Jesus is not a simple matter. But following him is still fundamentally the same as it has always been. It is a matter of returning again and again to what is truly important to living. It is a matter of a spiritual journey inward and a lifestyle journey outward. It is a matter of trust in the all sufficient grace and mercy of God. It is "basically" a matter of loving God completely and loving our neighbor as much as we love ourselves. On those two commandments everything we are or hope to be depends.

Matthew 23:1-12 (C, L, RC)
Matthew 23:1-13 (L²)

Proper 26 (C)
Pentecost 24², 26¹ (L)
Ordinary Time 31 (RC)

Who Is Greatest Among You . . .

How quickly we learn the desire to be great. The quest to become "number one" is a given in our competitive society. To some degree it is what fosters achievement and causes people to strive for excellence. Few people succeed without a fairly strong motivation to be foremost in their field. That's the positive side.

The negative side has to do with the absence of compassion and the undue pride that can go along with ambition. We can feel sorry for losers, but we prefer to associate with winners. Nothing pleases a student body more than a crucial victory by their team culminating in the chant, "We're number one; we're number one!" We look for and expect the recognition and reward that come with a promotion as we aim to move up another notch on the corporate ladder. And, if we end up disappointed with our advancement in life, well, we can still hope that our children will excel and achieve more than we did. It was the late coach of the Greenbay Packers, Vince Lombardi, who first coined the creed many would have to live by, "Winning isn't the only thing," he once said, "It's everything!"

Jesus had something to say about our need to get ahead. He didn't say that the desire to excel and achieve was wrong, but he did turn the tables on some common understandings of success. He redefined greatness, at least as far as our life in relationship with God is concerned.

One evening, I was on my way to a dinner meeting at a downtown hotel. I parked my car in the parking deck adjacent to the hotel and caught the elevator down to the street level. A big sales convention of some kind was in progress and three or four of the sales representatives rode down the elevator as I did. It was one of those elevators attached to the outside wall of the parking deck, with sides of glass, so you were afforded a bird's eye view of the whole area including the entrance to the hotel.

I could see a long black limousine parked at the entrance, complete with a uniformed chauffeur who was busily unloading a matched set of leather luggage from the trunk. A young man and woman were being escorted out of the limo and into the hotel. The whole scene exuded opulence, power, and notoriety. It also caught the eye of one of the sales representatives in the elevator, who nudged another passenger and in a serious tone said, "Look Joe, now there's a great salesman." Joe nodded in agreement, "Wow . . . ."

Whether the conclusion about this couple was accurate or not I don't know. Maybe the young woman was a great saleswoman. But, surely my fellow passenger spoke for a whole society in identifying what is commonly understood by success, achievement, and greatness.

The desire to be great is not confined to the business world or the athletic field by any means. Families compete with each other; children within a family may even vie for first place in the attention of their parents; and more than one parent has tried to live out some of their own unfulfilled dreams and goals vicariously through the achievements of their children.

Even churches want to succeed. And, more often than not, churches measure their greatness by benchmarks like attendance, budgets, size and condition of buildings, number of buses, size of staff, number of tithers, etc.

Success and the recognition it brings have been concerns of the church ever since there was a church. Even the first disciples of Jesus experienced some of the same feelings and needs for getting ahead that we have.

They must have felt at least a twinge of envy when they observed some of the Pharisees. Everybody recognized the Pharisees. Their phylacteries — small leather pouches containing bits of parchment inscribed with scripture — were always larger than necessary and their clothing distinctive. They revelled in recognition — seats at all the head tables, center front pews in church, being called "Doctor"and "Deacon" and "The Reverend." They were impeccably pious. They prayed ostentatiously before every meal; they carried their Bibles with conspicuous pride; they expected and received public credit for every donation; they lived for the applause of their admirers. Yes, few people would have denied that Pharisees were great men, and they were *all* men, not a female in their ranks.

But Jesus was not so impressed. It seemed to Jesus that though the Pharisees talked a good game, they were lousy players. Still, Jesus could see the envy in his disciples' eyes. After all, when the church across town becomes all the rage and garners the publicity, you can't help but wonder what's wrong with you and your kind. Everybody enjoys a little of the spotlight.

Sensing the opportunity for a word of instruction, Jesus sat down and called his followers to his side and began, "The scribes and Pharisees sit on Moses' seat . . ." Now that really caught their attention. That was precisely what they wanted — to be the greatest, to be the big cheese, top gun, to have the recognition and praise that go along with authority and power. So, they think "Keep talking Jesus; finish what you started to say; we're all ears!"

"The scribes and Pharisees sit on Moses' seat," Jesus continued, "but they do all their deeds so as to be seen by men . . . . You are not to be called rabbi . . . . Neither be called masters . . . . He who is greatest among you shall be your servant.''

Wait a minute . . . that wasn't what we expected, Jesus. We're confused. What kind of lesson in achievement was that? We were talking success here, not service; we thought you were going to tell us about power and popularity, not peasanthood.

How quickly the disciples had forgotten. Not too many days before they had come to Jesus asking, "Who is greatest in the kingdom of heaven?" and Jesus had placed a child in their midst. The child, he had said, was to be their model. Unless they became as children the doors to the Kingdom would never open. (Matthew 18:1-4) First-century society looked down on children. They were among the most vulnerable of all classes in society, often referred to as weak and dirty (due, in no small part, to the fact that the diaper had not yet been imagined!). Children had no rights, no respect, no recognition. To call them great in any sense was ludicrous.

How quickly the disciples had forgotten.

"Whoever is greatest among you shall be your servant." That must be remembered above all else. You must be willing to serve even the lowest, the least you can imagine. You must become as vulnerable as a child, because in God's Kingdom the measure of greatness is not the usual notion of success or achievement; it's service, and the humility of considering others before yourself.

Matthew doesn't give us a clue as to whether the disciples said a word. Maybe they were too embarrassed to speak. Sometimes an experience of truth has a way of rendering words unnecessary.

I think I know the feeling. When I was in college, there was on the campus a most distinguished professor. He was perhaps more esteemed and respected than any other teacher on the faculty, having received the distinguished teaching award so many times he practically owned the title. He taught religion, and, since it was a state university, all of his courses were electives; nobody was required to take any subject he offered. Yet, his classes were the most popular of all in the curriculum.

Students would sometimes sign up for one of his religious courses two or three semesters in advance just to be assured of a place in the class. If his classes were often closed because they were filled to capacity, his home remained opened, and students were always welcome there. He could call almost anyone in any of his classes by his or her first name — no small feat since his students numbered six or seven hundred per semester.

Although this professor lived within easy walking distance of his office, he frequently had his lunch at the school cafeteria in the heart of the campus. And like most school cafeterias, ours was a beehive of activity and noise.

Several students worked part-time in the cafeteria bussing tables and washing dishes so as to help pay tuition and other expenses. Made conspicuous by their white jackets, they worked feverishly during the noon hour trying to keep up with the influx of students all wanting a clean table instantly.

Unfortunately, a crudely callous tradition had developed there in the dining hall. Anytime one of the table servers would accidentally drop a plate or glass onto the floor, the students in the hall would burst into applause in a mocking gesture of recognition. More than once I saw a table server cower with embarrassment as he or she frantically tried to clear the broken china from the floor, while those enjoying their lunch clapped and laughed at them.

One particular noontime, the esteemed professor invited me and a couple other students to join him at his table for lunch. We quickly accepted the honor. While we were enjoying our student specials and some pleasant conversation, we heard a tremendous crash just a few feet behind us. Sure enough, one of the servers had slipped in the rush to clear a table and had dropped an entire tray of dirty dishes. Immediately the dining hall erupted with applause as the young man started to clean up the mess on the floor. He appeared to be on the verge of tears.

Then something happened that is indelibly impressed on my memory. Without saying a word, the professor stood up, walked over to the server who was frantically scraping up the mess on the floor, stooped down to his knees and began to help collect the broken glass and scraps of food and put them back on the tray.

The clapping stopped. And the dining hall fell silent as a morgue. For a few seconds we watched in disbelief and felt, ourselves, ashamed.

The dining hall tradition of mock applause died a well-deserved death that day, and we were taught more about true greatness in that one action than we could have learned in a semester of words.

If anyone would be great; if anyone would be "somebody"; if anyone would succeed and deserve recognition, then let him or her look at the masterteacher cleaning food from the cafeteria floor.

You're number one when you can embrace the lowest of the low and identify with their weakness and vulnerability. You're the greatest when you can see the pain and trouble in another's face and risk asking about it. You're a success when you can stick up for someone who is treated unjustly. You're really somebody when in silence you can sit by a bedside and hold a hand so another will not die alone. You're first when you don't mind being last for the sake of another.

And the church? Well, a church is great only to the extent that it serves the least and lowest of its community and world. It's such a simple lesson that Jesus taught. But somehow every time it's acted out, there falls a hush over all who see it.

Matthew 25:1-13 (C, RC)   *Proper 27 (C)*
Ordinary Time 32 (RC)

Life In The Meantime

The church has always lived between the times. We remember the time when Christ was born, died, and was raised, and we anticipate his return and the fulfillment of his Kingdom. In the meantime we live by faith in the truth of our memory and the certainty of our hope.

Likewise, every individual life is a meantime existence. We remember and learn from our past, and we anticipate some future expectation, the ultimate of which is life eternal. The meantime is the present, suspended between memory and hope. And to a large degree, realization of future hope is a matter of sensitivity to the demands and opportunities of the present moment.

Jesus often used parables to communicate the experience of that reality he called the Kingdom of God, a Kingdom which is also a meantime kind of existence. It looks back to its beginnings with the chosen Israel and forward to what theologians used to call its consumation. In the meantime, the Kingdom is, as John the Baptizer phrased it, "at hand." (Matthew 3:2)

Ten maidens have been asked to serve as wedding attendants. Theirs will be the honor of processing through the streets with the wedding party. The night of the wedding is a time of expectation and joy as the girls reminisce abut childhood days and former boyfriends and how they never thought Rachel would be the first among them to tie the knot. They gather their lamps, for soon it will be dark. Five of the girls are wise enough to realize that wedding rehearsals and weddings frequently run overtime, so they bring along some extra oil. The other five never give the possibility a thought.

As is often the case, someone gets lost on the way to the church or they just can't seem to get the tuxedos right, and so the groom and some of his ushers are late. Really late! So late that the girls fall asleep. Finally, some time later they are awakened by the minister shouting something about the groom not having a case of cold feet after all, he's finally here, the procession can begin.

The five maidens who were wise quickly replenish their dimly burning lamps with oil and rise to the occasion. But the five who brought no oil, unable to borrow from the wise maidens, must undertake a midnight scavenger hunt to find a dealer who will sell them what they need. While the foolish girls are out buying midnight oil the groom makes his appearance and they all take their places. When the five foolish maidens return to the church, they discover the service already in progress and the door closed and locked. Sadly, they miss out on the very thing to which they had looked forward for so long, and all the oil in the world cannot rekindle the light of joy in their hearts.

It is a tragic story about five maidens whose vision was so focused on the future that they failed to notice the demands of the present. They lived with a strong sense of expectation, and for that they should be commended, but they neglected to respond to the meantime in ways that would have equipped them to realize their hope.

For them, present time was for little more than just biding time. They did not understand its demands for preparation, sensitivity, and a readiness to act. When the meantime ran out, as it always does sooner or later, and the future came upon them suddenly, unexpectedly, they found themselves excluded because they were unprepared to respond. No doubt they protested vehemently that they were victims of circumstance. There was no way they could have known when the groom would appear. But their own rationalizations would have served only to seal their fate. They missed out on the very thing for which they had hoped.

That happens more often than we realize. So many folks live for the future to the exclusion of meaning in the present. One recent retiree confided one afternoon as we sat on his back porch, "All my working life I looked forward to retirement; I dreamed about the day it would come and what I would do; I sacrificed a lot to make it come as early as possible. Well, here I am, retired, and, I tell you what — it ain't what it's cracked up to be!"

Mind you, this little story Jesus told is no rehearsal of *carpe diem* philosophy. To the contrary, it says that we should understand that the present is part and parcel of the future. Like God's Kingdom which is coming but which is also here now, so we live in the meantime as though the future were already ours.

But think of the temptations we face in the meantime, temptations which rob the present of the meaning and joy God wants us to have. Whether that for which we hope is the second coming of Christ or fulfillment of some vision of personal happiness, think of the forces that use up our strength and leave us ill-prepared for real living. Weariness is a problem, especially when the thing for which we hope is so long coming (remember that all ten maidens, wise and foolish, fell asleep). What about frustration and anger when life doesn't take the turns we anticipate? Or, the loss of meaning that comes with apathy and failure of will? The meantime is filled with forces and experiences which can render us unable to embrace our hope when it comes upon us.

Moreover, the Gospel announces that hope has come upon us. The Kingdom is at hand. Whatever it may be that we hope for God to do in the future is present now, at least in part, for those persons who can see it and embrace it. No, we haven't witnessed the second coming, but we do have the Holy Spirit, who is Christ's coming now, daily. No, we do not enjoy world peace, but we do have a word of reconciliation which demands to be spoken now. Of course, none of us is entirely the person in Christ which he or she can be; all of us have rough edges and cluttered corners spiritually speaking. But, we do have a Lord, a Teacher, and his teachings are for now. And, to a large degree, the realization of whatever it is we hope for hinges upon our living in the present as though that future had arrived.

A few summers ago, I was a participant in a summer institute at St. Andrews University in Scotland. The last week of the institute coincided with the week the British Open Golf Tournament was being played on the Old Course at St. Andrews, a most pleasing coincidence for those of us who were addicted to the game.

At the close of one morning's lecture, an announcement was made that at two o'clock that afternoon a group of American golf pros would be arriving in the area on a chartered flight of a British Air Concorde. Additional advice suggested that we should assemble on a hill overlooking the Royal Air Force base across the bay if we wanted to see the Concorde land. Well, the flight of the Concorde and its arrival in sleepy St. Andrews was the talk of the luncheon tables, and almost all agreed that the event would be, or at least could be, the highlight of the afternoon.

So we gathered on the hilltop. Ladened with cameras, binoculars, and even a few folding chairs, we waited for the renowned supersonic air ship to break through the cloud cover. Time passed. At two-twenty, a few became bored and went into town shopping; at two-thirty, others found the ocean breeze a bit chilly and went to fetch a sweater; by two-forty-five, only a handful of people still waited on the hilltop, and a couple of them were asleep.

Finally, about three o'clock, someone yelled, "Look, look, there it is!" Like an enormous water fowl, it descended across the bay, nose tilted to afford the pilot a better view of the airstrip. It was majestic in its glide path, awesome in its speed and design. All of us cheered. We had seen the Concorde, and we were glad. It was worth the wait.

Maybe we were just in the right place at the right time, and others were not. Maybe we were just more patient, more willing to "waste some time" as someone suggested. Maybe we were just lucky.

Or, maybe the time of our waiting was really part of the whole experience. Maybe the anticipation, the looking and straining and imagining, was essential to our ultimate goal. Maybe it was the exciting event it turned out to be primarily because life in the meantime had been in itself a taste of what was to come.

Maybe it's the same with life in the Kingdom of God.

Matthew 25:14-30

Proper 28
Pentecost 25
Ordinary Time 33

In Defense of the One-Talent Servant
A sermon in drama

Narrator: For the next few minutes imagine that this sanctuary is a courtroom, and we are met to witness the trial of the one-talent servant. Usual courtroom rules and procedures have been altered and, in some cases, suspended altogether. Still, our aim is to hear the truth.

We have heard the familiar story of the one-talent servant in the reading of today's Gospel. It is a parable of the coming of God's Kingdom, a parable of God's judgment upon his servants, a parable about the nature of discipleship, of opportunity seized and lost.

The defendant is the one-talent servant who is accused of unfaithfulness in his position of steward or trustee of his master's resources. Because there is only one Judge capable of rendering a just decision in this matter, there will be no jury. And, of course, the Judge's decision is final.

Since the defendant's alleged offense is well-known by us as well as by the Judge, we will move directly to the defense of the accused. The defense attorney makes opening remarks.

Defense: Your honor, in due time we will demonstrate conclusively that the defendant is a decent, law-abiding citizen, respected in the community, and totally undeserving of the accusations brought against him. It will be made clear that this poor servant no more deserves harsh judgment than do all of us gathered in this courtroom today. Your honor, if the defendant is guilty, then we all are guilty, and the defense will show that this cannot be.

Narrator: The attorney for the prosecution waives opening remarks, so the defense begins the testimony by calling upon the first of three character witnesses. All are respected citizens who know the defendant well and can vouch for his honesty and integrity.

First Witness: Many's the time, your Honor, that I've loaned tools to this neighbor of mine. (The witness points to the defendant.) Not once has he failed to return them. Why, last summer while I was on vacation, the defendant deposited my weekly paycheck in the bank for me. I trust this man, your Honor; he's as honest as the day is long.

Second Witness: Your Honor, let me be candid. It's true that Brother One-Talent has not been the most active person in the church, but he has been a member virtually all his life, and his parents before him. The day the master had Brother One-Talent arrested, he used his one telephone call to notify the pastor what had happened. That just goes to prove how much the church means to him.

Third Witness: I'm the manager of the local bank, where Mr. One-Talent does his banking, your Honor. I see him often, and we've had some serious conversations over the years. One thing that has always impressed me about Mr. One-Talent is his concern for his family. "Charity begins at home," he would say, and nobody can deny that he took good care of the people in his home. They never went wanting for anything, so far as I know. If all my customers were like Mr. One-Talent, it sure would make my job in the bank a lot easier. Responsibility is his strong suit.

Narrator: Having established the defendant's reputation for honesty, church membership, and responsibility for his family, the defense now makes a dramatic move. A hush hurries through the hall as One-Talent is called to the stand to testify in his own behalf.

Defense: Mr. One-Talent, I know this will not be easy for you to do, but in your own words tell the court why you returned to your master only the one talent entrusted to your care.

One-Talent: (speaking in meek and tender voice, seeking to win over the minds and hearts of all present) Your Honor, I, well, I guess I was just afraid. Afraid I might fail. I'm not blessed with a lot of natural ability, your Honor. Oh, I can work alright; I'm not afraid of work. Ask anybody. But that one talent was it, all I had been given. You know how things are these days. The market goes up and down like a roller coaster; we have even seen some long-standing companies go under this year. Managing talents is risky business. There was a good chance that I could lose the whole talent. My master is known to be hardnosed about business matters. I mean, can you imagine his reaction had I reported the loss of even the one talent I had been given?

I'm only human, your Honor. I don't mind saying here today that I was scared — that's right, afraid of failing and coming up empty-handed. I couldn't live with that kind of disgrace. So I guess you could say, I tried to play it safe.

Defense: (speaking to the Judge) You see, your Honor, what pressure the defendant was under. In this topsy-turvy world, the defendant experienced the same fear that so many in this courtroom are feeling this very moment.

One-Talent: Being afraid is not against the law. I didn't hurt anybody, your Honor. I didn't cheat or embezzle. It's no crime to fall short of another person's expectations. What difference would my one talent have made in the whole scheme of things anyhow? If I had five or four or even two talents, well, that would be another matter. But I'm just a very small fish in a huge ocean, so what's the difference whether I do anything with my talent or not? Surely, I cannot be held accountable for what might have been. I might have lost everything. (The defendant struggles to maintain his composure.)

Defense: Your Honor, I realize that only Mr. One-Talent is on trial here today, but I think it is relevant to point out the current status of the other two servants who are in the employ of One-Talent's master.

As recent media reports have revealed, Five-Talent and Two-Talent both have been rewarded with handsome bonuses by their master. No one questions the superiority of their investment performance over that of the defendant. But that only underscores the need for compassion for the defendant.

Five-Talent and Two-Talent have had more to work with all their lives. And we all know it takes talent to make talent. The risk factor for them was not so great as for One-Talent. Had their investments gone sour, they could have withdrawn them before losing everything, but the defendant never had that kind of margin to play with.

Don't misunderstand me, your Honor, I'm not trying to pass the buck (or should I say "talent?"). But I feel compelled to note that Five-Talent and Two-Talent have had an easy life compared to the defendant.

One-Talent: (interrupting his attorney, speaking with emotion to the Judge) I only wanted to protect what I had. That's all. Is that so terrible? I'm no more guilty than everybody here.

Narrator: The silence in the courtroom is heavy with feeling as all who have come to the trial realize that they could easily be the defendant in this case. Their emotion is a mixture of pity and grief. And, in the context of such drama and pathos, the defense rests its case.

The lawyer for the prosecution rises to speak. The prosecutor's voice is filled with honest compassion as he/she addresses the defendant.

Prosecution: Mr. One-Talent, you are right. We are afraid, all of us. Afraid of many things, some known, mostly unknown. But we also know that, demanding as your master may be, the master has never condemned anyone for failure, only for an unwillingness to try.

One-Talent, your master did not ask you to return five talents, or even two. Your master asked only for what you were given with interest, with that additional amount that would have naturally accrued if you had given it half a chance.

Your master never instructed you to protect your talent, but to use it. Your master never advised you to play it safe in the game of life, but to play it with faith. Your master is not nearly so concerned with the quantity of your results as with the quality of your efforts.

One-Talent, as much as it pains me to say it, your error is the tragic mistake of trying to live by your own standards of security and safety instead of risking and venturing all for the sake of your master.

Narrator: With those few brief statements, the prosecution rests its case, and all eyes focus on the Judge. There is obvious strain evident in the Judge's face and voice. It appears that the judgment to be made is one which weighs heavily upon the Judge's heart. Finally, the Judge speaks.

Judge: The defendant will rise. Mr. One-Talent, I understand your fear that you may lose all you have. But you fail to recognize that what you have is not really yours. What you have is a gift, entrusted to you by your master.

Yes, it is true that your resources are limited, but whatever you have, be it great or small, is important and needed, and therefore must be used and nurtured. One-Talent, people of our faith *are* responsible for the potential we have been given.

Our God calls us for what we can become as well as for what we are.

Others do have more talent than do you, One-Talent. But don't you see, you cannot excuse your own lack of faith and poor stewardship because of the strength or weakness of others. You are responsible for yourself.

You say that you wanted to protect what belonged to your master. One-Talent, surely you must realize that your master does not want or need your protection; your master wants your faith and trust put into action.

And now, servant, you say that you are sorry. So am I. Opportunities lost are seldom regained. Eventually time runs out on opportunities to put your love and faith into action. Your master will never run out of talents to give you, but you and I and all of us will run out of time to use them.

It grieves me to judge you, One-Talent, but you bring this judgment upon yourself. You are guilty. And neither your tears, nor even the tears of God, can recall what was lost.

Narrator: With the pronouncement of the verdict, there is a collective gasp in the audience. Some even object audibly that the verdict is unfair. But the Judge's gavel strikes the desk and the objections give way to weeping and gnashing of teeth.

In the midst of the surprise and anguish, however, at least one thought from the Judge's words lingers in the people as they return to their homes and jobs, "God calls us not only for what we are, but also for what we can become." Becoming more than we are in terms of faith or love or discipleship means that we must risk what we are now. Growth means risk and adventure, not safety and protectiveness. It may be too late for One-Talent, but not for us.

Matthew 24:1-14　　　　　　　　　　Pentecost 27 (L)

Promise or Threat?

"Wars and rumors of wars," Jesus said. Nation against nation, kingdom against kingdom, famines, earthquakes, tribulation, even death sentences for the faithful, wickedness multiplied, and all the while the Gospel is preached around the world — these are some of the signs of Christ's second coming and the end of the age. Tell me, would you consider his words a promise or a threat?

My first recollection of any mention of Christ's second coming goes back to when I was six or seven years old. My grandfather was taking me somewhere in his 1949 Hudson — probably one of the ugliest cars ever made, but it rode like a dream! It was getting close to Christmas, close enough that I had already made the longings of my heart known to Santa Claus. I was hoping for a bicycle that year, a shiny red one, with chrome fenders, and plastic streamers on the handlebar grips that would flutter in the wind, sleek and fast. Santa Claus had taken due notice of my request, and I had checked it out with those who would eventually pay Santa's bill and they had agreed, so in my mind the plans for the bike were complete. Nothing else to do but wait.

As we rode along in my grandfather's Hudson, I noticed that frequently he would lean forward toward the windshield and look up into the sky in front of us. I looked too. The sky was mostly clear and bright with stars and a nearly full moon. Here and there a few clouds.

"Look," my grandfather said, "look at the moon." It had a pinkish hue and around it a rather hazy looking ring. It seemed strange and eerie.

My grandfather contined, "When the moon looks that way, I wonder if it's time for the rapture?"

"What's a rapture?" I asked him.

"When Christ will come again and take us all to be with him in heaven. Jesus said there would be signs in the sun and moon and stars. Maybe this is one of them."

I was pretty quiet for a while after that. And, I remember thinking to myself, "Lord, if you really are coming again, could you please wait until after Christmas?"

Ever since that evening, the thought of the second coming has always evoked a little fear and anxiousness on my part. I guess my enjoyment of life, imperfect as it is now, causes some sadness at the thought of it all being changed.

There are lots of different feelings, questions, doubts, and misunderstandings concerning this teaching of the Bible. More than a few preachers have used Christ's words about the second coming as a kind of threat to try to scare folks into conversions. Still others dismiss the doctrine altogether as outdated and irrelevant. After all, we've seen a person walk on the moon. So we think that scientific minded, post-lunar-landing-people like us shouldn't be too concerned with a biblical image which pictures Christ coming amidst signs in sun and moon and stars. Reports of famine and earthquake are hardly news anymore. And as for turmoil among nations, has any generation lived in a time of total world peace? So, with those conclusions and questions, few of us give the matter any serious thought. But, should we?

Our appreciation and understanding of the message at the heart of the doctrine of second coming would be enriched, I think, if we could hear it anew through the ears of the early Christians, the people who wrote the New Testament, the people to whom this teaching was first given.

In order for us to do that, I need your help. The success of this sermon from this point on is going to depend in large part upon you and your imagination. I need your imagination for just a few minutes.

I want you to imagine that due to a critical shortage of natural resources, the whole world, and this country in particular, becomes the scene of radical political upheaval. Try to imagine that because the very survival of the human race is severely threatened, it becomes necessary for the people of this country to submit themselves to radical changes in our government. We soon find ourselves living under a kind of dictatorship, with the government making all the decisions about allocation of resources, decisions about who shall have what food and how much, decisions about who shall live and who shall not. Most of our personal freedoms are taken away or at least restricted.

In an effort to keep people in line with government policy and action, it is decreed that there shall be only one religion, and the new dictator will be head of the new church. Local traditions like lovefeasts and the sacraments and worship in our own sanctuary are strictly forbidden. Complete conformity to the rules of the new religion created by the government is demanded of everyone.

But, let's also imagine that we refuse to give up our faith and our practice of worship. We know the risk involved, but still we agree to continue to meet secretly for worship and fellowship as Christians. In spite of fear and harrassment, and even an occasional arrest of one of our members, we covenant with each other to carry on with the practice of our beliefs.

Now imagine that one Friday afternoon, just before the workday ends, you are informed that all Christians, including yourself, should not bother to report for work on Monday. It seems that your employer can no longer withstand the pressure from the government and the penalties it imposes upon any company which employs Christians.

So you turn towards home in a state of shock over the events of the day, only to receive another jolt from your children as you sit around the dinner table. They relate to you how, that same day, uniformed officials gave a talk in their classroom about the foolishness of following the old traditions and then announced that they would return on Monday to hear reports on just how many of their parents had secretly disobeyed the law over the weekend by meeting with others for worship.

All day on Saturday there are periodic news bulletins on radio and television describing the deteriorating state of affairs throughout the world. Wars and conflict, threats and upheavals as people fight for scarce resources. Your impression is that virtually all of the institutions of your society are under attack or suspicion and many are being transformed to serve more effectively the new government.

Early Sunday morning there is a knock at your door. You answer and are confronted by a grim-faced official who announces that you will have to go with him; there are questions you must answer. So you are taken away, placed under arrest, and finally locked in a cell. You ask about the charges against you and are told bluntly that the only charge is treason — treason by virtue of illegal religious expression.

So there you are, separated from your loved ones and friends, your life in disorder, your future highly foreboding. You long for the way things used to be, and the memories of lost laughter and happiness play across your mind like a cinema.

Can you bear up under the hopelessness of your situation? Will you be strong enough in faith? What will become of your loved ones? Is this to be the reward of a life of faith in Jesus Christ?

Now, one last effort of imagination. Given those circumstances, given that feeling of longing and a desperate desire for a better world, would it not be possible, even probable, that the sincerest prayer in your heart would be, "Even so, Lord Jesus, come; come quickly? Return now, Lord, and set the world right; deliver your people from the awful plight and persecution under which they live."

Depending in part upon how good an imagination you have, perhaps you now understand why for the Christians of the late first century, the biblical teachings about the second coming were held to be a source of great hope and consolation. For many of them were experiencing persecutions much like those we have tried to imagine. We can understand in part at least that Jesus' instruction concerning signs of distress and conflict among nations, and wickedness multiplied, was intended not so much to scare his followers or even to convert unbelievers, but to strengthen and encourage the faithful lest they give in to hopelessness in a time of trial.

But of course the end did not come as many of them expected. It still hasn't. The signs have been with us for generations — wars and rumors of wars, nation rising against nation. In terms of signs of the end, the church has always lived in a world that looked to be in its last days.

Edmund Steimle once pointed to the statue of the Angel Gabriel atop the roof of Riverside Church in New York City. There the angel is poised, horn to his lips, ready to break forth with a mighty blast in announcement of Christ's return. Through ice and sleet, heat and cold, summer rain and winter storm, there Gabriel is perched ready to sound the call. And as Steimle said it, ". . . but there is no mighty blast. Not even a tentative toot." (from a sermon, "The God of Hope" in *Disturbed by Joy*, Fortress Press, Philadelphia, 1967, p. 14.) Yet in terms of signs, the city beneath the steeple has always lived in the last days.

So what should we conclude? Given the delay in Christ's return, what must we do? The answer is found in the words of our Lord himself. He says, "But he who endures to the end will be saved." (v. 13)

The New Testament Greek word translated "endure" literally means, "to stand one's ground in affliction." It means to remain steadfast and not give up even in the face of difficult odds. The answer is to persist in faith and hope. The answer is to believe that no suffering or heartache can last forever. The answer is to confront the gloom and doom of this life with the assurance that Christ's Kingdom will ultimately be victorious. Though heaven and earth pass away, God's word of promise lives on eternally.

Even when, especially when, your world is falling apart, you, Christians, must keep the faith, for God will come and save you.

This is a major note in the song of the Gospel. Take heart amidst the sorrow and sadness of this world and behold the light of God's promise to come and transform life.

In these troubled times, troubled as much or more than have been any times, it takes a full measure of faith to persevere in work and prayer and hope for those qualities of life which reveal God's Kingdom. But the Kingdom belongs to those who endure when the signs of the times seem to say that faith is futile and hope is foolish. The promise is ours that though the earth shake and the heavens tremble, the love of Christ shall ultimately triumph over all evil and sin. So we stand our ground in the face of affliction.

Of course we live in the last days. We always have and always will, but that's meant to be a sign of hope, not fear. And that same hope infuses the present age with purpose and gives life abundant to all who believe. Take heed that no one leads you astray with false prophesies and threats about signs of the end. Our Lord has given us a promise, not a threat. And the promise is that all who remain steadfast in faith, hope, and love, will be saved. Let it be so with us.

Matthew 25:31-46
(Ezekiel 34:11-16, 23-24)

Proper 29 (C)
Christ the King (L)
Ordinary Time 34 (RC)

God's Safety Net

Political jargon over the last decade has given us a new understanding of an old term. The term is 'safety net.'

My first recollection of a safety net was at the Ringling Brothers and Barnum and Bailey Circus when it was still performing under the big top. Who could forget those daring acrobats balanced on the trapeze or high wire and, under them, a net. When the act was finished they would fall gracefully from their lofty perch into the open arms of the net, a kind of tease, I suppose, a hint of the terror of even the slightest slip or false step. Occasionally there was a daredevil who would work without a net, and the drum would roll, and people would gasp, a few would scream. I never saw a performer injured in a real fall, although I have read that it happens. Today, with the cement and hardwood floors of most coliseums, working without a net is virtually unheard of. It's just as well — a person with skill doesn't have to risk life and limb to be entertaining.

But in our newest fashion of speech, a safety net has come to stand for that last resort of protection and assistance provided by government for people who are otherwise helpless and vulnerable. The continuing debate is not over whether or not we should have such a social safety net, but how much is necessary and for whom. The questions have to do with how much or how little responsibility a nation has for those who cannot help themselves, and who they are.

The Scripture given for today, the Festival of Christ the King, addresses a similar matter — the concern of Christ, the Judge of the nations, for the welfare of persons who cannot be self-supporting but who must rely on the compassion and generosity of others. Of course, that concern includes all of us to some extent, because every person is dependent upon others. Nobody is completely self-sufficient. It's really just a matter of degree.

The prophet Ezekiel, writing almost six hundred years before Christ, was distraught that the leaders, or "shepherds," of Israel had taken advantage of the weak and had devoured the very sheep they were supposed to tend. Thus, the prophet envisions a day when God will personally shepherd the people of Israel, a day when there will be a Good Shepherd who will care for and feed the flock with justice and tenderness, not avarice and greed.

Ezekiel's imagery is vivid. The Good Shepherd will seek the lost and bring back the recalcitrant sheep who keep going astray. The Good Shepherd will bind up the injured and crippled sheep, strengthen the fearful and weak. The Good Shepherd will watch over the fat and strong sheep, so that they do not take advantage of the lean and weak ones. The Good Shepherd will act as judge, and will be especially watchful to see that as the sheep graze in a pasture they do not trample the grass around them and thus spoil it for others. The Shepherd Judge will act to be certain that sheep who drink from a stream do not jump into the water with their feet and thus foul the water for those who must drink it farther down the bank (ecology is not a new concern). Finally, says Ezekiel, the Good Shepherd will control the fat sheep, that is the strong and robust sheep, to see that they do not thrust at the weak with their horns in order to threaten and intimidate them.

All this, says the prophet, God will do through an appointed shepherd whom God will send, a servant like David who will guarantee that in Israel there is a safety net for those who are hanging by their fingernails to the bottom rung of the socioeconomic ladder.

Six centuries later, in the imagery of the last judgment, Jesus assumes the role of Ezekiel's Good Shepherd/Judge. The nations of the world are assembled before the enthroned Shepherd/Judge who divides them, sheep from goats, based on the nations' responses to the lowest or least of persons in their societies.

Jesus' final concern for the least of his brothers and sisters is not surprising. He had an affinity for the poor, the outcasts, the dregs of society, and they seemed to have gravitated toward him as well. In the imagery of the last judgment, Jesus goes so far as to suggest that he is so identified with human need that the way we respond to the needy of the world is the way we respond to the Lord himself. It would appear that the Lord of the church is saying to those who are the church that we are to be, in some sense, God's safety net. How much more plain could it be said than in this parable that the church's love for Christ will be realized or lost by our efforts to feed and clothe and shelter and console? The world is filled with persons who are unprotected, uncared for, hungry, abused, and belittled, and Christ the King is looking for his church to be their support, the embodiment of a God who is Refuge and Strength.

But, as plain as Jesus makes it, we are left to wrestle with the question of how. How do we feed and shelter and console? Our inability to come to any kind of consensus in answering that question has divided the church and has pushed some Christians to try to wash their hands of the whole problem and retreat into a religion of purely "spiritual" focus. Because of the magnitude and complexity of the problems of hunger, poverty, and injustice in our world, still other Christians have concluded that the question is purely individualistic, so that as long as you and I are socially concerned and responsive as individuals we have done all we are called to do and be. This conclusion ignores Ezekiel's interest in the welfare of the *whole flock* of Israel, and Jesus' own vision of the last judgment being of *nations* and their responses to humanity.

To put it succinctly, the world is in a mess, and there are few signs that we are even gaining ground on the crises of hunger and poverty. In depressed moments a person could justifiably conclude that our world is heading toward a multiple choice end, the choices being: (a) starvation, (b) nuclear holocaust, (c) environmental collapse, or (d) all of the above! Furthermore, the church, called as it is to feed and clothe and shelter, is frequently as much a part of the problem as of the solution.

But the answer is not despair! None of the sheep in the parable of the last judgment was excused because she or he gave up hope and quit. Notwithstanding the complexity and magnitude of the problem, there are steps the church can take. The weaving of a safety net is our task even it if must begin with small stitches.

Some joker once suggested that the likelihood was that, in the Parable of the Good Samaritan, the priest and the Levite who passed by on the other side of the road and left the injured traveller dying in the ditch were probably on their way to their congregation's World Missions Committee meeting! As cynical as that suggestion may be, it does remind us that we have to reckon with the close-at-hand world we live in and its needs. Let's call it our small world of direct personal accountability. No matter how big or grand our concern for the whole world, that concern is somehow pitiable if it overlooks the needs of persons in our own backyards, our own cities and neighborhoods and congregations. So, the first step we can take in fashioning God's safety net is to work on an attitude which is sensitive and responsive to the people who hurt next door and across town.

In this small personal world where the effect of our action is fairly direct, there are fat sheep and lean sheep, and there are sheep who try to horn in on the rights of others, and there are sheep who foul the water which others have to consume and trample the pasture upon which others must feed. We have a responsibility (an important word in Matthew's understanding of the Gospel) within our personal world of influence to see that the weaker ones among us are not abused or treated unjustly. Christian adults have a responsibilty to see that their children know not only The Lord's Prayer, but also the Lord's priorities — the concern for the welfare of all humankind. That responsibility is better modeled than taught. When personal comfort and happiness become the consuming motivation of a church, the gospel words of the last judgment will fall on deaf ears or drift away into soothing sentimentalism. What will not go away is our accountability — yours and mine. I am personally accountable for my response to the human beings over which I have some direct influence, and I need to get my own personal house in order. I am painfully reminded of the church which launched a congregation-wide program for world famine relief while two members of its janitorial staff tried to support their families on the minimum wage!

A second step toward becoming the safety net God wants us to be moves us beyond our small worlds of direct influence and into the big world of power and politics. Many folk choose to drop out of the march when this step is called for. It's a step into the realm toward advocacy for the poor, the outcasts, the persecuted, the sick and homeless. It's a step into the realm of power politics and populations of people we will never see face to face and whose plight we will never fully understand. The answers to the problems of human need in this larger world is not for us to dole out food and clothes, although we must do that until an answer is constructed, but to be advocates for new political structures and economic systems which will feed and clothe and protect.

Think of the frequency with which the Scriptures remember Jesus as an advocate for people who were vulnerable and at the mercy of the decisions of others. A woman tried and convicted of the capital offense of adultery, children whom the disciples considered a bothersome interruption to the agenda of the day, a woman who annointed Jesus' feet with perfume and incurred the criticism and belittling of others in the house — for all of these and others like them, Jesus was not only a religious high priest, but also a social advocate and defender. He did it time after time. The Lord of the least and little came to the defense of the defenseless.

And so does his body the church. We are now the advocates, the defenders of the defenseless, the protectors of the vulnerable, the voice of those whom the powers of the world will not hear. Through our influence and power in the institutions of government, church, education and business, we are meant to be the good shepherds who watch over the sheep. Modern-day shepherds 'tend' their sheep in ways Ezekiel never dreamed of — becoming knowledgeable, organizing, voting, boycotting when needed, writing public officials and policy makers, and speaking out when it's risky. The safety net is woven in a multitude of ways.

Finally, there is a third response to this complex world of human need. We can, all of us, pray for it.

Intercessory prayer can be used as a cop-out, a way of easing a guilty conscience without lifting a finger to offer aid or advocacy. But *real* intercession, not the kind that offers God a shopping list of requests, but the kind that offers God one's *self*, is the church's unique responsibility. When we pray for the fulfillment of the needs of others in our world, that prayer is also a self-offering by which those who pray offer themselves as part of the answer to the prayer.

Our intercessions are not for the purpose of persuading God or providing God with needed information. God is not some cosmic computer whose power switch is off until our prayers turn it on. Our intercessions are offerings of our love, faith, and resources to the end that we might become instruments of God's answer to the very prayer we make.

Be prepared for that. Among the costliest prayers are genuine intercessions for one's church or country, or of a spouse for her or his partner, of a parent for a child, a friend for a friend. We may discover that we become the direct bearer of our prayer's answer. That is always true with prayer which is self-offering.

Drawn from Jesus' parable of the last judgment, I have this mental image of a scene filled with surprises. Not the least of those surprises will be the presence in heaven of persons nobody expected to be there (even some who did not themselves expect to be there) and maybe the absence of some whom everybody assumed would be first in line. Among those surprises will be our Lord, the Shepherd King, saying, "Come close to me, you who have loved me; for you fed me and clothed me and consoled me; you stood up for me when I was weak. You defended me when I was vulnerable; you spoke up for me when no one would listen; you offered yourself for me in your prayers."

And the faithful will say, "You must be mistaken, Lord. As much as we might wish we had, we simply never did all that. How could we feed or clothe or console *you?* You are above human need. How could we pray for you when you are our Intercessor before the Father? We never did that for you."

"O but you did," the Shepherd King will say, "for inasmuch as you did for the least and lost and lonely, the little and the limited, you did for me. So come close to me, for you see I still desire the touch of those who care."

John 8:31-36   **Reformation Day/Reformation Sunday**

The Freedom of Necessity

"If you continue in my word, you are truly my disciples, and you will know the truth, and the truth will make you free."

Like most teenagers I looked forward to my sixteenth birthday as a day of liberation. Being sixteen meant that I could get a driver's license, and the open road of freedom and self-determination would be mine for the taking. At last, I thought, I could be my own person, no longer dependent on parents or older friends to take me where I wanted to go. My sixteenth birthday would be "Independence Day," "Bastille Day," the day of liberation.

A couple of days before that long-awaited anniversary, I was with my family as we returned home from an evening out. I don't remember where we had been, but it was nearing midnight when the four of us turned onto the highway leading to our house.

Rounding a sharp curve we were startled by flashing red lights in the road ahead. Police vehicles, ambulances, and the sounds of voices magnified by walkie-talkies were everywhere. We had arrived only minutes after a terrible wreck. I remember feeling ill at the moment and wondering whether the accident involved my neighbor and classmate who had received a driver's license just a few weeks before.

We continued on our way home, but the next morning's news gave the tragic details of what had taken place. Two drivers, who were both sixteen, were racing, filling both lanes of the narrow road. They met another car head-on around the curve. The result was two teenagers seriously injured and a family of three dead.

My enthusiasm for getting a driver's license suffered a severe blow that night. The realization came to me in the worst sort of way that the freedom I longed for, with all its independence and personal privileges, was just the flip side of a serious responsibility. The open road of freedom was also the narrow path of obligation.

A similar realization is suggested in Jesus' words to us about being made free by the truth. The truth which liberates us is none other than the truth of God in Jesus Christ, the knowledge of which comes through discipleship. Jesus is proclaiming that freedom comes not through independence, but through dependence upon him and his word. The Bible never speaks of freedom as "doing things our way" or "doing our own thing." Sadly, some people spend lifetimes searching for that vague "something" which will enable them to sing along with Frank Sinatra, "I Did It My Way," but end up slaves to their own wants and desires, slaves to sin, as the Gospel calls it. Fred Buechner describes it this way, "It is to feel, inside our own lives, as helpless to escape as slaves are helpless, because the one thing we can't escape is ourselves." (*A Room Called Remember,* San Francisco, Harper and Row, 1984, p. 110.)

Freedom in the knowledge of Christ is release from bondage to the self and, at the same time, the recognition of a new master. Freedom is found through living under orders, the order of the Cross. It is the freedom of necessity, the necessity to follow Christ.

On Reformation Sunday, we Christians of the Protestant persuasion pay homage to the reformers who are our forebears. We praise their boldness and their will to protest even at a cost of considerable personal sacrifice. We remember stories of persecution and imprisonment. Yet even in times of abuse or physical bondage, the reformers were free in a way that their oppressors were not. Theirs was a freedom of necessity. They had been encountered by the truth and that truth impelled them to speak, to write, to act, to love. Their freedom was not a state of independence but one of obligation and responsibility to continue in the Word of Christ, that is, to be disciples.

The witness of a black pastor in South Africa comes to mind. He had been "detained" by the authorities on numerous occasions, arrested, jailed, and interrogated without any charges being filed. One of the detentions had lasted several months, during which time he was physically tortured. Hearing how boldly he continued to preach, I asked him whether or not he was afraid. He replied, "Yes, at first I was afraid, afraid of the pain, the separation from my family. But once their interrogation began, I thought to myself, 'They are the ones who live in houses with bars on the windows and doors; they build high fences around their property and keep guard dogs in their yards and guns in their closets.' And it suddenly came to me that they were the ones who were afraid. And just as suddenly, I was not afraid anymore." This pastor was free from fear in a way his interrogators could never imagine, and his freedom issued forth from his bondage to Christ and to the liberating word of the Gospel.

So it is with the freedom of necessity, the freedom that comes from knowing the truth of God revealed in Jesus Christ. It is the liberty not to do as we please, but to do as pleases God. It is a freedom in which all rights are also obligations and all obligations are privileges. Along side the Magna Carta, the Bill of Rights, or any other great document of human liberty, the Word of Christ to love God completely and one's neighbor as oneself stands as the key which unlocks the human spirit and breaks the chains that would bind a person to a lesser loyalty.

The lives of the great pioneers of faith are inspiring. From Pastor Martin Luther of Wittenburg to Mother Teresa of Calcutta there is a compelling witness to the freedom that comes in knowing Christ, a freedom manifested in selfless giving without counting the cost.

But of equal inspiration to me are the lives of less famous, more common folk I meet everyday. These are the men and women who, indifferent to the social pressures to be seen among the "right" people in the "right" places, are perfectly free to go where the need is greatest and embody the love of Christ. These are the everyday saints and reformers who are free to love and serve people regardless of which side of the tracks they are from or how much money they make or what color their skin. These are the liberated folk for whom the chains of prejudice, peer pressure, and popularity have been cut loose. They live with a knowledge which supercedes everything else they know or believe. They know the truth, and that truth has placed them under a liberating necessity.

To them the doors to the Kingdom open wide. Theirs is a share of the blessing of the Gospel, a blessing against which all other privileges pale in comparison. They are God's own free people, Kingdom people, and daily you and I are invited to stand among their number with the promise, ". . . if the Son makes you free, you will be free indeed."

Matthew 5:1-12   All Saints' Day/All Saints' Sunday (C, L)

When the Poor Become Rich

"Blessed are the poor in spirit; for theirs is the kingdom of heaven."

Bumper sticker philosophy would have us believe that there are many sources of happiness. Some say, "Happiness is surfing," or "Happiness is a glass of cold milk," or even, "Money can't buy happiness, but happiness can't pay the bills."

Unfortunately, bumper stickers seldom capture the whole truth. Nobody can say for certain what formula of circumstances guarantees happiness. If we could, given the market for such a product, we could write the formula in a book and retire independently wealthy.

The whole truth must include the reality that happiness is illusive. Although surveys show that most people consider themselves to be happy persons, few people, if any, are happy all the time. Furthermore, most people admit to a desire to be happier than they are presently. But as to what causes a person to be happy, who can say for sure?

In his novel, *Dr. Fischer of Geneva,* Graham Greene reflects on the subject in this way:

> *But how does one convey happiness? Unhappiness we can so easily describe — I was unhappy, we say, because . . . We remember this and that, giving good reasons, but happiness is like one of those islands far out in the Pacific which has been reported by sailors when it emerges from the haze*

where no cartographer has ever marked it. The island disappears again for a generation, but no navigator can be quite certain that it only existed in the imagination of some long-dead lookout.
(Graham Greene, *Doctor Fischer of Geneva or The Bomb Party,* New York, Simon and Schuster, 1980, p. 53)

As understood in the Bible, happiness is the condition of being spiritually blessed. It is an inner assurance of God's love and grace; it's a confidence in God's eternal care. Misunderstanding is likely if we confuse the biblical state of blessedness with our common notions of happiness which, for the most part, are descriptions of good feelings dependent upon surrounding circumstances. Jesus was not suggesting that those who mourn should feel good about their mourning or that those who suffer persecution should enjoy their trials. Rather, in his beatitudes, Jesus was offering assurance of divine grace and care to those who experience the uncertainties and sorrows of life. They are truly blessed who, in the midst of personal pain or sacrifice, can still rejoice in the unfailing love of God. Within a century after the death and resurrection of our Lord, the church would be referring to itself and especially to its martyrs as "blessed" or "happy." They were blessed, not because they enjoyed an easy, undemanding life, but because they possessed an inner conviction of God's presence despite stormy conditions and treacherous times.

The year was 1735 when a young Englishman, fresh from study at Oxford, and feeling a divine call to do missionary work in the colony of Georgia, boarded a ship for Savannah. There he would take up the challenge of ministry to immigrants and Indians. But within days he found himself face to face with death. A ferocious Atlantic storm engulfed the small ship. The vessel was tossed and broken as wave after wave washed across the deck, and disaster appeared imminent. As with so many others on their way to the colonies, it seemed that all on board would be listed, "lost at sea."

While fear and panic spread among the passengers and crew, the young Oxford fellow noticed a small group of men and women huddled together, calmly praying, singing hymns, and speaking words of comfort one to another. He was deeply touched by their faith and courage.

Amazingly (some would say miraculously), the storm passed, and the ship was spared with no loss of life. The young Englishman approached the small band of women and men and inquired as to the reasons for their calm in the face of such grave danger. He learned that they were members of the religious society of Moravians, also destined for Savannah, also determined to establish a mission and a church. And the source of their quiet confidence? Why, nothing less than the assurance of the love and grace of the Savior, they told him.

The young man was so impressed by their witness of action and word that sometime later, when he returned to London thoroughly discouraged and disillusioned, he sought out the fellowship and support of the Moravian congregation meeting at Fetter Lane. In the course of time he would experience new purpose and direction for his life, culminating at a study group meeting at Aldersgate when his heart was "strangely warmed."

The young Englishman was John Wesley, of course, and from the work of his mind and hands and the inspiration of his heart came the great churches of the Wesleyan tradition, including the United Methodist Church.

Wesley's experience with the Moravians on board ship and similar experiences of many other people gave the eighteenth century Moravians a reputation as "God's happy people." To some, this happiness was evidence of naivete, even childishness, but to others — John Wesley among them — it was a witness to the blessedness promised by Christ, a spiritual happiness given to those who mourn, to the meek, the merciful, those who search for righteousness, the pure in heart, peacemakers, and persecuted. Happy are all those people, because God has not abandoned them; God is their comfort and strength.

Moreover, the blessedness promised by Jesus is not a happiness we can create, it is a gift of God. The first of Jesus' beatitudes is indicative of this essential character of all the rest.

"Blessed are the poor in spirit." With that seemingly modest opening Jesus begins his pronouncement of blessings. "Poor in spirit" is likely to conjure up images of beggars and persons who are down and out, objects of pity for others around them. "Poor in spirit" — if a person introduced to us were so described, how likely would we be to seek out that person as a friend? "Poor in spirit" — if he applied for a job as a salesman, would we hire him? If she wanted to be a minister of the Gospel, would we ordain her? If we were looking for spiritual mentors or models, would we consider people who had the reputation of being poor in spirit? Probably not.

Yet, being poor in spirit is the beginning of blessedness, says Jesus. And we wonder how that could possibly be so.

Poor in spirit has little or nothing to do with personality type or with the strength of one's devotional life or even with one's depth of commitment. It involves what a person expects of God and the kind of attitude a person brings to life itself. An attitude which is poor in spirit is unassuming and undemanding before God. It rejoices simply in God's love and grace without placing conditions upon that faith. Jesus is promising God's blessing to those persons who live day-by-day dependent upon divine grace, not resting upon the laurels of their own righteousness. The poor in spirit are always the meek, the merciful, the seekers of God, the pure in heart, the peacemakers, and frequently the persecuted. They know their own spiritual poverty, thus they can feel empathy for those around them who also struggle. They can trust God unconditionally, because they know God's love for them is unconditional.

Arthur Rubenstein is reported to have claimed, "I accept life unconditionally. Most people ask for happiness on condition, but happiness can only be felt if you don't set any condition." The poor in spirit set no condition, thus any moment in life, regardless whether it be a time of elation or sorrow, is for them a moment when God is present. Any relationship is one in which God is at work. Any circumstance of life is one which God can redeem. Nothing is able to separate them from the love of God in Jesus Christ, thus in all things their aim is solely to please God, to be opened to receive his love, to experience the happiness of knowing that life is a gift. They are seldom disappointed by life, for it brings to them far more happiness than they could ever earn or achieve by their own striving. For the poor in spirit, sorrow and pain are real and not to be denied, but they are not afraid or without hope, for they ask, "If God is for us, who is against us?" (Romans 8:31) These are the meek who inherit the earth. Theirs is the blessed assurance. They place their trust in a God who owes them nothing, but who gives them all they truly need, even the Kingdom of Heaven.

Maybe the illusiveness of happiness is the result of some of the conditions we set. Ask yourself what it is that would make you truly happy or even happier than you are now. A better paying job? A bigger house? Being more loved or needed? Having a family life as perfect as the Huxtables on the Cosby Show? A second home? The perfect husband or wife? Two kids and a station wagon with a sheep dog in the back? What would it take?

There is no end to the conditions we may think are essential, and these conditions can become the terms on which we either accept life or become critical of it and the way it treats us. Then we may find ourselves disappointed when the terms are not met, or even when they are, the brief happiness they bring may quickly disappear into the haze like that island in the ocean.

When Jesus sat down to teach his disciples about happiness he spoke of blessedness of spirit, not conditions of circumstance. He taught that true happiness grows from an unconditional acceptance of life as the good gift of a gracious God, a God whose all-consuming purpose is to bless us and, in all circumstances, to make us the objects of his love. God so blesses, not because he owes us anything, but because his very nature compels it.

Happiness is . . . ? It's many things, we think, as the years go by. But when the years come to their end, it may be none of the things we thought. The Gospel says that happiness is one thing only — it's being so poor in spirit as to realize how truly rich we are in the love and grace of God.

About the Author

A native of North Carolina, Wayne Burkette has served as an ordained minister of the Moravian Church for twenty years, all in his home state. His longest pastorate was as Senior Pastor of the historic Home Moravian Church in Old Salem, Winston-Salem, where he served for thirteen years. In 1985 he was named Senior Pastor of Fairview Moravian Church, also in Winston-Salem — a city which is a center for the Moravian Church in the southeastern part of the United States. His pastorates have been marked by a strong emphasis on worship, preaching, and congregational renewal. From 1982-84 he was liturgist for the well-known Easter Sunrise Service of the Salem Moravian Congregation.

He was a recipient of a John Motley Morehead Scholarship to the University of North Carolina at Chapel Hill, graduating with a bachelor's degree in psychology in 1966. He received a M.Div. degree from Moravian Theological Seminary, Bethlehem, Pennsylvania and a D.Min. from Union Theological Seminary, Richmond, Virginia. He also has studied in the Graduate School of Education at Wake Forest University and the Institute for Mediterranean Studies, Jerusalem, Israel. In connection with church assignments and continuing education, he has travelled extensively in England, Europe, and southern Africa.

From 1983-89, Dr. Burkette was an elected member of the Provincial Elders' Conference (Executive Administrative Board) of the Moravian Church in America, Southern Province, holding the office of Vice-President from 1986-89. In addition to service on numerous other denominational boards and commissions, he continues to be active in community organizations and causes.

During the past two years, Dr. Burkette has written for the Church School curriculum series, *Celebrate* and *Bible Discovery*. He also has contributed sermons and articles published in *Pulpit Digest, Christian Ministry, Clergy Journal* and *The Moravian* magazine, and has conducted workshops in homiletics and goal-setting for local congregations. He is married to the former Nancy Witherspoon of Jefferson, North Carolina, and they have two teenage daughters.